AI 2042: A Vision for Tomorrow's Technology

AI SERIES 3

Erkan YILDIRIM

Table Of Contents

01

Chapter 1: Introduction to AI2042

The Evolution of Artificial Intelligence

In the subchapter "The Evolution of Artificial Intelligence" in the book "AI 2042: A Vision for Tomorrow's Technology," we explore the incredible journey of AI from its humble beginnings to its current state of sophistication. Artificial Intelligence has come a long way since its inception, with rapid advancements in machine learning, neural networks, and deep learning algorithms propelling it forward. As software developers and programmers, it is crucial to understand this evolution in order to harness the full potential of AI in our tech creations.

For tech entrepreneurs and gadget lovers, the evolution of AI presents exciting opportunities for innovation and disruption. From virtual assistants like Siri to self-driving cars, AI has already made a significant impact on our daily lives. However, the future of AI goes far beyond these applications, with the potential to revolutionize industries such as healthcare, finance, and transportation. By staying informed about the evolution of AI, entrepreneurs and early adopters can position themselves at the forefront of this technological revolution.

Students and young professionals entering the field of AI must be aware of its evolution in order to stay competitive in the job market. As AI continues to advance, the demand for skilled professionals in this field is only expected to grow. By studying the evolution of AI and gaining hands-on experience with cutting-edge technologies, students can set themselves up for a successful career in this rapidly expanding industry.

For policymakers and government officials, understanding the evolution of AI is crucial for creating effective regulations and policies. As AI becomes more integrated into society, issues surrounding data privacy, security, and ethical implications will become increasingly important. By staying informed about the evolution of AI, policymakers can make informed decisions that balance innovation with societal well-being.

Economists, sociologists, parents, philosophers, ethicists, and the general public all have a stake in the evolution of AI. The impact of AI on the economy, society, ethics, and daily life cannot be understated. By examining the evolution of AI from multiple perspectives, we can better understand its potential benefits and risks, and work towards a future where AI serves humanity in a responsible and ethical manner.

Current Applications of AI

In the subchapter "Current Applications of AI" in our book "AI 2042: A Vision for Tomorrow's Technology," we explore the diverse range of ways in which artificial intelligence is being utilized in the present day. From healthcare to finance, education to entertainment, AI is making a significant impact on various industries and aspects of our daily lives. This subchapter aims to provide insight into the cutting-edge applications of AI that are shaping our world today.

One of the most prominent applications of AI is in healthcare, where it is being used to diagnose diseases, personalize treatment plans, and improve patient outcomes. AI-powered medical imaging technology, for example, can help doctors detect tumors, fractures, and other abnormalities with greater accuracy and efficiency. In addition, AI algorithms are being developed to predict and prevent diseases before they manifest, revolutionizing the field of preventive medicine.

In the financial sector, AI is being employed to analyze vast amounts of data to detect fraudulent activities, predict market trends, and automate trading processes. AI-driven chatbots and virtual assistants are also being used to enhance customer service and streamline banking operations. By leveraging AI technologies, financial institutions are able to improve decision-making, reduce risks, and increase operational efficiency.

In the realm of education, AI is being used to personalize learning experiences, assess student performance, and provide targeted interventions to help students succeed. Adaptive learning platforms powered by AI algorithms can cater to individual learning styles and pace, making education more engaging and effective. AI tutors and virtual classrooms are also being developed to provide students with personalized support and guidance.

In the entertainment industry, AI is being utilized to create immersive experiences, generate personalized recommendations, and streamline content production processes. AI algorithms are used to analyze viewer preferences and behaviors to recommend movies, songs, and TV shows tailored to individual tastes. In addition, AI-powered tools are being used to automate tasks such as video editing, sound mixing, and special effects, enabling filmmakers and content creators to work more efficiently.

Overall, the current applications of AI are vast and diverse, showcasing the potential of this technology to transform various industries and aspects of society. As we continue to innovate and push the boundaries of AI technology, it is essential for us to consider the ethical implications and societal impact of these advancements. By staying informed and engaged, we can ensure that AI is used responsibly and ethically for the betterment of humanity.

The Impact of AI on Society

Artificial Intelligence (AI) has become an integral part of our daily lives, impacting various aspects of society in profound ways. From improving efficiency in businesses to revolutionizing healthcare and transportation, AI has the potential to shape the future of technology. As software developers and programmers, it is crucial to stay updated with the latest AI trends and advancements to stay ahead in this rapidly evolving field.

Tech entrepreneurs and gadget lovers are increasingly exploring the possibilities of AI in creating innovative products and services. Whether it's developing smart home devices or designing AI-powered robots, the potential for AI to enhance our everyday lives is limitless. Early adopters are eagerly embracing AI technology, paving the way for a future where AI seamlessly integrates into our daily routines.

Students and young professionals are recognizing the importance of AI skills in today's job market. As AI continues to disrupt various industries, having a solid understanding of AI principles and applications can open up numerous career opportunities. Policymakers and government officials are also grappling with the implications of AI on society, from regulating AI algorithms to addressing ethical concerns surrounding AI technologies.

Economists and sociologists are studying the impact of AI on labor markets and income inequality. As AI automation becomes more prevalent, there are concerns about job displacement and the need for upskilling the workforce to adapt to the changing job landscape. Parents are also concerned about the role of AI in their children's education and development, from AI-powered tutoring systems to ethical concerns about AI bias and data privacy.

Philosophers and ethicists are engaging in debates about the ethical implications of AI, from the moral responsibility of AI systems to the potential for AI to surpass human intelligence. As AI becomes more advanced, questions about AI consciousness and the boundaries between humans and machines are becoming increasingly relevant. The general public is also becoming more aware of the impact of AI on society, from AI-driven social media algorithms to concerns about AI surveillance and privacy. Overall, the impact of AI on society is far-reaching and multifaceted, requiring a collaborative effort from various stakeholders to ensure that AI technologies are developed and deployed responsibly.

Overview of AI 2042

AI 2042 is set to revolutionize the way we interact with technology in the near future. This subchapter provides an overview of the advancements and potential applications of artificial intelligence in the year 2042. From software developers and programmers to tech entrepreneurs and gadget lovers, this information is crucial for anyone interested in staying ahead of the curve in the rapidly evolving field of AI.

One of the key highlights of AI 2042 is its ability to go beyond the current capabilities of virtual assistants like Siri and self-driving cars. The advancements in AI technology have paved the way for more personalized and efficient interactions with machines, leading to a more seamless integration of AI into our daily lives. This will open up new possibilities for businesses and individuals looking to leverage AI for various applications.

Students and young professionals will find AI 2042 particularly relevant as they prepare to enter the workforce of the future. Understanding the potential impact of AI on various industries will help them stay competitive and adapt to the changing technological landscape. Policymakers and government officials will also benefit from this information as they work to regulate and govern the use of AI in a way that maximizes its benefits while minimizing potential risks. Economists and sociologists will find AI 2042 to be a fascinating glimpse into the future of work and society. The rise of AI is expected to have profound implications for job markets, income inequality, and social dynamics. By understanding the potential outcomes of AI 2042, these experts can better prepare for the economic and social changes that lie ahead. Parents, philosophers, and ethicists will also find this information valuable as they consider the ethical implications of AI technology and how it may impact future generations.

In conclusion, AI 2042 represents a new frontier in technology that promises to reshape the way we live, work, and interact with the world around us. By staying informed about the advancements in AI technology, individuals from all walks of life can better prepare for the future and harness the potential benefits of AI in their own lives. Whether you are a software developer, tech entrepreneur, student, policymaker, economist, or simply a curious member of the general public, AI 2042 offers a glimpse into the exciting possibilities that lie ahead in the field of artificial intelligence.

02

Chapter 2:
Advancements in AI
Technology

Quantum Computing and AI

In recent years, the fields of quantum computing and artificial intelligence (AI) have been rapidly evolving, leading to exciting possibilities for the future of technology. Quantum computing, in particular, has the potential to revolutionize the way we approach complex computational problems by harnessing the power of quantum mechanics. This emerging technology has the ability to solve problems that are currently intractable for classical computers, making it a game-changer for a wide range of industries.

One of the most promising applications of quantum computing is in the field of AI. By leveraging the unique properties of quantum systems, such as superposition and entanglement, researchers are exploring new ways to enhance the capabilities of AI algorithms. Quantum AI has the potential to significantly improve the speed and efficiency of machine learning tasks, enabling us to develop more advanced AI systems that can tackle complex problems with ease.

For software developers and programmers, the integration of quantum computing and AI presents a host of exciting opportunities. By gaining a deeper understanding of quantum principles and learning how to apply them to AI algorithms, developers can create more powerful and efficient software solutions. This will not only lead to advancements in existing AI technologies but also pave the way for entirely new applications that were previously impossible to achieve with classical computing alone.

Tech entrepreneurs and gadget lovers alike are eagerly anticipating the convergence of quantum computing and AI. As these two technologies continue to evolve and intersect, we can expect to see a wave of innovative new products and services entering the market. From quantum-powered AI assistants to intelligent quantum sensors, the possibilities are endless for those who are willing to explore the frontiers of technology.

In conclusion, the fusion of quantum computing and AI has the potential to reshape the technological landscape in profound ways. As policymakers, economists, and sociologists consider the implications of these advancements, it is crucial that we approach this new era of technology with a thoughtful and ethical mindset. By working together to harness the power of quantum AI for the greater good, we can build a future where innovation and progress go hand in hand, benefitting society as a whole.

Neural Networks and Deep Learning

In the subchapter "Neural Networks and Deep Learning" of the book "AI 2042: A Vision for Tomorrow's Technology," we delve into one of the most exciting and transformative technologies of our time. Neural networks are at the core of many artificial intelligence systems, enabling machines to learn from data and make decisions in a way that mimics the human brain. Deep learning, a subset of neural networks, has revolutionized industries ranging from healthcare to finance, and continues to push the boundaries of what is possible with AI.

For software developers and programmers, understanding neural networks and deep learning is essential for staying at the forefront of technology. These tools are being used in everything from image and speech recognition to natural language processing and self-driving cars. By mastering the principles behind neural networks, developers can create more powerful and efficient AI systems that can solve complex problems and improve our lives in countless ways.

Tech entrepreneurs and gadget lovers will find that neural networks and deep learning hold immense potential for creating innovative products and services. From personalized recommendation systems to predictive analytics, these technologies enable businesses to better understand their customers and anticipate their needs. By leveraging the power of neural networks, entrepreneurs can unlock new opportunities for growth and disruption in their respective industries.

Students and young professionals interested in AI and machine learning will benefit greatly from studying neural networks and deep learning. These technologies are driving the next wave of innovation and are in high demand across a wide range of job markets. By gaining expertise in neural networks, students can set themselves up for successful careers in fields such as data science, robotics, and software engineering.

For policymakers, economists, sociologists, and ethicists, understanding the implications of neural networks and deep learning is crucial for addressing the ethical, social, and economic challenges that come with AI advancement. As these technologies become more integrated into our daily lives, it is essential to consider the potential impacts on privacy, security, and inequality. By engaging in thoughtful discussions and debates, policymakers can help shape the future of AI in a way that benefits society as a whole.

Natural Language Processing

Natural Language Processing (NLP) is a critical area of artificial intelligence that focuses on the interaction between computers and human language. In the context of AI 2042, NLP plays a crucial role in enabling machines to understand, interpret, and generate human language in a way that is both meaningful and contextually relevant. This subchapter will delve into the advancements and applications of NLP in the rapidly evolving landscape of technology and society.

For software developers and programmers, NLP presents a myriad of opportunities to create innovative applications that can revolutionize the way we interact with technology. From chatbots and virtual assistants to language translation and sentiment analysis, the possibilities are endless. By harnessing the power of NLP, developers can build intelligent systems that can understand and respond to human language with unprecedented accuracy and efficiency.

Tech entrepreneurs and gadget lovers will also find NLP to be a fascinating area of exploration. As AI continues to permeate every aspect of our lives, NLP will play a key role in shaping the future of human-machine interaction. Whether it's enabling more natural and intuitive communication with our devices or facilitating seamless language translation across borders, the potential for NLP to transform the way we interact with technology is truly limitless.

Students and young professionals looking to enter the field of AI will find NLP to be a captivating and challenging domain. By mastering the intricacies of NLP, aspiring technologists can position themselves at the forefront of innovation and play a role in shaping the future of technology. The demand for skilled NLP experts is only expected to grow in the coming years, making it a valuable skill set for those looking to make a meaningful impact in the field of AI.

Policymakers, economists, sociologists, and ethicists will also need to grapple with the implications of NLP on society at large. As AI technologies continue to advance, questions around privacy, security, bias, and ethics will become increasingly complex and nuanced. By engaging in thoughtful and informed discussions about the societal implications of NLP, these stakeholders can help shape policies and regulations that ensure the responsible and ethical development and deployment of AI technologies.

Robotics and AI Integration

In the rapidly evolving landscape of technology, the integration of robotics and artificial intelligence (AI) has become a pivotal focus for researchers, developers, and industries alike. This subchapter delves into the intricacies of how these two cutting-edge technologies are coming together to shape the future of tomorrow's technology.

Robotics, traditionally associated with physical automation and mechanical tasks, has now entered a new era of sophistication with the incorporation of AI. By leveraging AI algorithms and machine learning capabilities, robots are becoming more intelligent, adaptable, and autonomous than ever before. From industrial robots on factory floors to collaborative robots working alongside humans in various settings, the possibilities are endless.

The fusion of robotics and AI is not only revolutionizing the way we work and interact with technology but also raising important ethical and societal questions. As we witness the rise of robots with human like features and cognitive capabilities, questions surrounding job displacement, privacy concerns, and ethical dilemmas come to the forefront. It is imperative for policymakers, economists, sociologists, and ethicists to collaborate in shaping regulations and guidelines to ensure the responsible deployment of these technologies.

For software developers and programmers, this integration presents a plethora of opportunities to innovate and create groundbreaking applications that can enhance efficiency, productivity, and user experience. Tech entrepreneurs and gadget lovers can explore new avenues for product development and market disruption by leveraging the power of robotics and AI. Students and young professionals entering the field of technology are encouraged to embrace this convergence as they prepare for a future where AI and robotics will be ubiquitous.

As we navigate this exciting yet complex terrain of robotics and AI integration, it is essential for the general public to stay informed and engaged. By understanding the implications and potential benefits of these technologies, we can collectively shape a future that is both technologically advanced and ethically sound. AI 2042 envisions a world where robotics and AI work in harmony to create a more efficient, sustainable, and inclusive society for generations to come.

03

Chapter 3: Ethical Considerations in AI 2042

Bias and Fairness in AI Algorithms

In the rapidly evolving world of artificial intelligence, the issue of bias and fairness in AI algorithms has become a topic of great importance and concern. As we continue to rely more and more on AI technology in our daily lives, it is crucial that we address and mitigate any biases that may be present in these algorithms. Bias in AI algorithms can arise from a variety of sources, including the data used to train the algorithms, the design of the algorithms themselves, and the way in which they are implemented. For example, if a facial recognition algorithm is trained primarily on data from one demographic group, it may struggle to accurately recognize faces from other groups. This can lead to serious consequences, such as misidentifying individuals or perpetuating stereotypes. Ensuring fairness in AI algorithms is essential to building trust in these technologies and preventing harm to individuals and communities. Developers and programmers have a responsibility to carefully consider the potential biases that may be present in their algorithms and take steps to address them. This may involve diversifying the training data, testing the algorithms for bias, and implementing measures to mitigate any biases that are identified.

Tech entrepreneurs and gadget lovers must also be aware of the potential biases in AI algorithms and advocate for fairness and transparency in the development and deployment of these technologies. By demanding fair and unbiased AI algorithms, we can help ensure that these technologies benefit society as a whole, rather than perpetuating existing inequalities. Overall, addressing bias and fairness in AI algorithms is a complex and challenging task that requires collaboration and input from a wide range of stakeholders. By working together to identify and mitigate biases in AI algorithms, we can help ensure that these technologies are used ethically and responsibly, and that they benefit all members of society.

Privacy and Security Concerns

In the rapidly advancing world of artificial intelligence privacy and security concerns have become a top priority for software developers and programmers tech entrepreneurs gadget lovers early adopters students young professionals policymakers government officials economists sociologists parents philosophers ethicists and the general public As we delve deeper into the realm of AI technology it is crucial to address the potential risks and implications associated with the collection and use of personal data

One of the primary concerns surrounding AI technology is the protection of sensitive information With the increasing reliance on AI powered devices and applications there is a growing risk of data breaches and cyberattacks Software developers and programmers must prioritize the implementation of robust security measures to safeguard user data and prevent unauthorized access Additionally tech entrepreneurs and gadget lovers should be vigilant in choosing AI products and services that prioritize privacy and encryption

Furthermore as AI technology continues to evolve there is a heightened concern about the potential misuse of personal data for targeted advertising and manipulation Policymakers and government officials play a crucial role in establishing regulations and policies to ensure that AI systems are used ethically and transparently Economists and sociologists can provide valuable insights into the societal impact of AI technology on privacy and security while philosophers and ethicists can offer ethical frameworks for guiding the development and deployment of AI systems For parents it is essential to educate children about the importance of privacy and online safety when interacting with AI powered devices By instilling good digital habits early on parents can help protect their children from potential risks and vulnerabilities Additionally the general public must stay informed about the latest advancements in AI technology and actively participate in discussions about privacy and security concerns

In conclusion as we look towards the future of AI technology in 2042 and beyond it is imperative that we address privacy and security concerns with the utmost diligence and responsibility By working together to prioritize data protection transparency and ethical decision making we can ensure that AI technology serves as a force for positive change in our society Let us strive to create a future where privacy and security are paramount in the development and deployment of AI systems

Accountability and Transparency in AI Systems

In the fast-paced world of artificial intelligence (AI), accountability and transparency are crucial components for ensuring that AI systems are developed and deployed responsibly. As we look towards the future of technology in AI 2042, it is imperative that we prioritize these principles to build a more ethical and trustworthy AI ecosystem.

Accountability in AI systems refers to the responsibility that developers and organizations have in ensuring that their AI technologies are fair, unbiased, and safe for users. This means being transparent about how AI algorithms are trained, the data they are fed, and the potential biases that may exist within the system. By holding developers and organizations accountable for the outcomes of their AI systems, we can prevent harmful consequences and promote greater trust in AI technology.

Transparency in AI systems is equally important, as it allows users to understand how AI algorithms make decisions and why certain outcomes are produced. Transparency enables users to question, challenge, and hold AI systems accountable for their actions. By making AI systems more transparent, we can empower users to make informed decisions about the technology they interact with and ensure that AI is used in a responsible and ethical manner.

As software developers and programmers, it is our responsibility to prioritize accountability and transparency in the AI systems we create. By implementing ethical design principles, conducting thorough testing and validation processes, and regularly auditing AI systems for biases and errors, we can help build a more responsible AI ecosystem. Additionally, collaborating with policymakers, economists, sociologists, and ethicists can help us navigate the complex ethical challenges that arise in AI development and deployment.

In conclusion, accountability and transparency are essential pillars for building a more ethical and trustworthy AI ecosystem in AI 2042 and beyond. By prioritizing these principles, we can ensure that AI technology is developed and deployed in a responsible manner that benefits society as a whole. As we continue to innovate and push the boundaries of AI technology, let us remember the importance of holding ourselves accountable and being transparent in our efforts to create a better future for all.

Ethical Decision-Making in AI Development

Ethical decision-making in AI development is a crucial aspect that must be carefully considered as we continue to push the boundaries of technology in the 21st century. In the book "AI 2042: A Vision for Tomorrow's Technology," we delve into the complexities of creating artificial intelligence systems that not only enhance our lives but also adhere to ethical principles that uphold human values and rights. This subchapter is dedicated to software developers and programmers, tech entrepreneurs, gadget lovers and early adopters, students and young professionals, policymakers and government officials, economists and sociologists, parents, philosophers and ethicists, and the general public who are curious about the future of AI beyond Siri and self-driving cars.

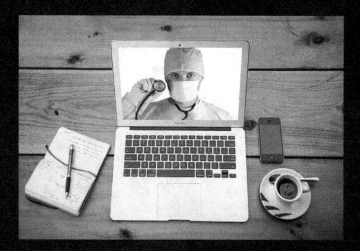

As we advance in AI technology, it is imperative for developers and programmers to consider the ethical implications of their creations. From biased algorithms to privacy concerns, the decisions made in the development process can have far-reaching consequences on society as a whole. By actively engaging in ethical decision making, developers can ensure that their AI systems are designed with fairness, transparency, and accountability in mind.

Tech entrepreneurs and gadget lovers are often at the forefront of adopting new AI technologies. It is essential for this audience to understand the ethical considerations that come with incorporating AI into their products and services. By prioritizing ethical decision making, tech entrepreneurs can build trust with their customers and contribute to a more ethical and responsible AI ecosystem.

For students and young professionals entering the field of AI development, it is crucial to be aware of the ethical challenges that come with creating intelligent systems. By engaging in discussions around ethical decision making, these individuals can learn how to navigate complex ethical dilemmas and contribute to the development of AI systems that align with human values and rights.

Policymakers and government officials play a vital role in shaping the regulatory landscape for AI development. By understanding the ethical implications of AI technology, policymakers can create policies that promote the responsible use of AI and protect individuals from potential harms. It is essential for policymakers to collaborate with experts in ethics and technology to ensure that AI development is guided by ethical principles.

In conclusion, ethical decision making in AI development is a critical component of creating a future where AI technologies benefit society as a whole. By considering the perspectives of software developers and programmers, tech entrepreneurs, gadget lovers and early adopters, students and young professionals, policymakers and government officials, economists and sociologists, parents, philosophers and ethicists, and the general public, we can work together to build a more ethical and responsible AI ecosystem in the years to come.

04

Chapter 4: The Future of AI2042

AI in Healthcare and Medicine

In recent years, artificial intelligence (AI) has made significant strides in transforming the healthcare and medicine industries. The integration of AI technology in these sectors has led to a plethora of advancements that have revolutionized the way healthcare professionals diagnose, treat, and manage patient care. From predictive analytics to personalized medicine, AI has the potential to greatly improve patient outcomes and reduce healthcare costs.

One of the key areas where AI has made a significant impact is in diagnostics. AI algorithms have been developed to analyze medical images, such as X-rays, MRIs, and CT scans, with a level of accuracy that rivals or even surpasses that of human experts. This has not only improved the speed and accuracy of diagnoses but has also led to earlier detection of diseases, ultimately saving lives. Additionally, AI-powered diagnostic tools can help healthcare professionals make more informed decisions about treatment options, leading to better patient outcomes.

Another area where AI is transforming healthcare is in personalized medicine. By analyzing vast amounts of patient data, AI algorithms can identify patterns and trends that can help predict which treatments will be most effective for individual patients. This personalized approach to medicine has the potential to revolutionize the way we treat diseases, moving away from a one-size-fits-all model to one that is tailored to each patient's unique genetic makeup and lifestyle factors.

AI is also being used to improve patient care and management. Virtual health assistants powered by AI can help patients manage their medications, track their symptoms, and communicate with healthcare providers. These virtual assistants can provide patients with personalized healthcare advice and reminders, ultimately improving patient adherence to treatment plans and leading to better health outcomes.

As we look to the future of healthcare and medicine, it is clear that AI will play an increasingly important role in shaping the industry. From improving diagnostics to personalizing treatment plans, AI has the potential to revolutionize healthcare in ways we have never seen before. It is crucial for software developers, tech entrepreneurs, policymakers, and the general public to stay informed about these advancements and work together to ensure that AI is used ethically and responsibly in the healthcare sector.

AI in Education and Learning

In the realm of education and learning, artificial intelligence (AI) has the potential to revolutionize the way we acquire knowledge and skills. With the rapid advancements in AI technology, educators are increasingly turning to AI-powered tools to personalize learning experiences, provide real-time feedback, and enhance overall student engagement. From virtual tutors to adaptive learning platforms, AI is reshaping the landscape of education in ways that were once unimaginable.

One of the key benefits of AI in education is its ability to tailor instruction to the individual needs of each student. Through the use of algorithms and machine learning, AI can analyze a student's learning patterns and preferences to create a personalized learning path. This not only helps students learn at their own pace but also ensures that they are receiving the support and resources they need to succeed. Additionally, AI can provide instant feedback on assignments and assessments, allowing students to track their progress and make improvements in real time.

AI-powered tools are also revolutionizing the way educators assess student performance and provide support. By analyzing data from student interactions with digital learning platforms, AI can identify areas where students are struggling and intervene with targeted interventions. This proactive approach to student support can help prevent learning gaps and ensure that all students have the opportunity to reach their full potential. Furthermore, AI can assist teachers in grading assignments, freeing up valuable time for more meaningful interactions with students. For tech entrepreneurs and gadget lovers, the possibilities of AI in education are endless. From interactive learning games to virtual reality simulations, AI-powered tools are transforming the way we engage with educational content. As AI continues to evolve, we can expect to see even more innovative solutions that cater to different learning styles and preferences. Whether you are a student looking to enhance your learning experience or a parent seeking educational resources for your child, AI in education offers a wealth of opportunities for growth and development. As we move towards a future where AI plays an increasingly prominent role in education, it is crucial for policymakers, economists, and sociologists to consider the implications of this technology on society as a whole. Issues such as data privacy, equity in education, and the impact of automation on the workforce are just a few of the challenges that must be addressed as AI continues to reshape the education landscape. By engaging in thoughtful discussions and considering the ethical implications of AI in education, we can ensure that this technology is used responsibly and ethically for the benefit of all.

AI in Business and Industry

AI in Business and Industry is revolutionizing the way companies operate and make decisions. In the past, businesses relied on human intuition and experience to drive their strategies. However, with the advancements in artificial intelligence, organizations now have access to powerful tools that can analyze vast amounts of data and provide valuable insights. This has led to increased efficiency, productivity, and profitability across various industries.

Software developers and programmers play a crucial role in implementing AI technology within businesses. They are responsible for creating algorithms and systems that can automate tasks, predict outcomes, and optimize processes. By leveraging AI solutions, companies can streamline their operations, reduce costs, and gain a competitive edge in the market. Tech entrepreneurs and early adopters are also at the forefront of this revolution, as they are constantly seeking new ways to integrate AI into their products and services.

Students and young professionals are increasingly recognizing the importance of AI skills in today's job market. With the rise of automation and machine learning, having a strong foundation in AI can open up a world of opportunities in various industries. Policymakers and government officials are also paying close attention to the impact of AI on the economy and society. They must navigate the complex ethical and regulatory challenges that come with deploying AI technologies in business settings. Economists and sociologists are studying the long-term implications of AI on job markets, income inequality, and social structures. While AI has the potential to create new jobs and industries, it also raises concerns about job displacement and the concentration of wealth in the hands of a few. Philosophers and ethicists are exploring the moral implications of AI in business and industry. As machines become more autonomous and decision-making processes become increasingly opaque, questions of accountability, transparency, and fairness come to the forefront.

Overall, AI in Business and Industry is a dynamic and evolving field that requires collaboration and innovation from a diverse set of stakeholders. Whether you are a software developer looking to build cutting-edge AI applications, a policymaker navigating the regulatory landscape, or a concerned citizen pondering the ethical implications of AI, it is essential to stay informed and engaged in the ongoing dialogue surrounding AI technology. By working together, we can harness the power of AI to create a more prosperous, equitable, and sustainable future for all.

AI in Entertainment and Recreation

AI in entertainment and recreation is revolutionizing the way we consume and interact with media. From personalized recommendations on streaming platforms to virtual reality gaming experiences, artificial intelligence is enhancing our entertainment choices in ways we never thought possible. In the world of AI 2042, entertainment will be more immersive, interactive, and tailored to individual preferences.

One of the most exciting applications of AI in entertainment is the development of virtual companions and characters. These AI-driven entities can engage with users in real-time, creating unique and dynamic experiences in video games, movies, and virtual reality simulations. Imagine playing a game where the NPCs (non-player characters) respond to your emotions and adapt their behavior based on your actions. This level of interactivity is made possible by advances in AI technology. Furthermore, AI is being used to create hyper-realistic special effects in movies and TV shows. Gone are the days of clunky CGI - with AI, filmmakers can produce lifelike characters and environments that seamlessly blend into live-action footage. This not only saves time and money in the production process but also opens up a world of creative possibilities for storytellers.

In the realm of music and art, AI algorithms are helping to generate new and innovative content. From composing original music to creating stunning visual art pieces, AI is pushing the boundaries of creativity and expression. Artists and musicians are collaborating with AI systems to produce work that transcends traditional boundaries and challenges our perceptions of what is possible in the realm of entertainment.

As we look to the future of AI in entertainment and recreation, it is essential to consider the ethical implications of these technologies. How do we ensure that AI-driven content is inclusive, diverse, and respectful of cultural sensitivities? How do we protect user data and privacy in a world where AI algorithms are constantly analyzing our preferences and behaviors? These are just a few of the questions that policymakers, ethicists, and the general public must grapple with as AI continues to transform the way we consume and create entertainment.

05

Chapter 5: Challenges and Opportunities in AI 2042

Job Displacement and Reskilling

In the rapidly evolving landscape of technology, job displacement and reskilling have become crucial topics of discussion. As artificial intelligence (AI) continues to advance, many industries are facing the reality of automation and the potential loss of jobs traditionally held by humans. This subchapter aims to explore the impact of AI on the workforce and the importance of reskilling in preparing for the future.

One of the key challenges posed by AI is the displacement of jobs that can be automated by machines. This includes tasks that are repetitive, predictable, and rule-based, which are often found in industries such as manufacturing, retail, and customer service. As AI technologies become more sophisticated, the potential for job displacement increases, leading to concerns about unemployment and economic inequality. It is essential for policymakers and government officials to address these challenges and implement strategies to support displaced workers.

Reskilling plays a vital role in mitigating the effects of job displacement caused by AI. By acquiring new skills and adapting to the changing demands of the labor market, individuals can remain competitive and secure employment in emerging industries. This requires a proactive approach to education and training, with a focus on developing skills that are in high demand in the digital economy. Software developers and programmers, tech entrepreneurs, and students and young professionals must stay abreast of the latest technological trends and continuously update their skill sets to stay relevant in the job market.

For parents and educators, it is important to prepare the next generation for the future of work by promoting a culture of lifelong learning and adaptability. By instilling a growth mindset and fostering curiosity and creativity, young people can develop the resilience and skills needed to thrive in an AI-driven world. Additionally, policymakers and economists must collaborate to create policies that support reskilling initiatives and ensure that workers have access to quality education and training programs.

In conclusion, job displacement and reskilling are complex issues that require a multi-faceted approach involving collaboration between government, industry, and academia. By acknowledging the challenges posed by AI and investing in reskilling initiatives, we can create a more inclusive and sustainable future for all members of society. It is essential for all stakeholders, including software developers and programmers, tech entrepreneurs, policymakers, and the general public, to work together towards a shared vision of a future where technology enhances human potential and prosperity.

Regulation and Governance of AI

In the rapidly evolving landscape of artificial intelligence (AI), the regulation and governance of this powerful technology have become paramount concerns for a wide range of stakeholders. From software developers and tech entrepreneurs to policymakers and ethicists, the need for clear guidelines and oversight mechanisms has never been more pressing. In this subchapter, we will explore the current state of AI regulation and governance, as well as potential future directions for ensuring the responsible development and deployment of AI technologies. One of the key challenges in regulating AI is the rapid pace of innovation in this field. As AI systems become more advanced and capable of autonomous decision-making, questions arise about accountability and liability for their actions. Policymakers and government officials must grapple with these complex issues to ensure that AI technologies are used ethically and responsibly. This includes considerations of data privacy, algorithmic bias, and the impact of AI on society as a whole.

For software developers and programmers, navigating the regulatory landscape can be daunting. Different countries and regions have varying approaches to AI regulation, creating a patchwork of rules and standards that can be difficult to navigate. However, adherence to best practices and industry guidelines can help developers ensure that their AI systems meet ethical and legal requirements, while also fostering innovation and growth in the AI industry. Tech entrepreneurs and early adopters of AI technologies must also be aware of the regulatory environment in which they operate. Failure to comply with regulations can result in costly fines and reputational damage, making it essential for businesses to stay informed about the latest developments in AI governance. By proactively engaging with regulators and policymakers, tech entrepreneurs can help shape the future of AI regulation in a way that promotes innovation and protects consumers.

In conclusion, the regulation and governance of AI are complex and multifaceted issues that require collaboration and dialogue among a diverse set of stakeholders. By working together to develop clear guidelines and oversight mechanisms, we can ensure that AI technologies are used ethically and responsibly, benefiting society as a whole. As we look towards the future of AI in 2042 and beyond, it is essential that we lay the groundwork for a regulatory framework that fosters innovation while safeguarding against potential risks and harms.

International Cooperation in AI Development

In the subchapter "International Cooperation in AI Development," we explore the importance of collaboration between countries in the advancement of artificial intelligence technology. As AI continues to evolve and shape the future of technology, it is crucial for nations to work together to ensure its responsible and ethical development. By sharing knowledge, resources, and best practices, countries can accelerate progress in AI research and innovation.

Software developers and programmers play a key role in this international cooperation, as they are at the forefront of AI development. By collaborating with their peers from around the world, developers can exchange ideas, collaborate on projects, and drive innovation in the field of AI. This collaboration not only benefits individual developers but also contributes to the overall advancement of AI technology on a global scale.

Tech entrepreneurs and gadget lovers are also important stakeholders in international cooperation in AI development. By working together with innovators from different countries, entrepreneurs can access new markets, expand their networks, and create cutting-edge AI products and services. Gadget lovers and early adopters can benefit from this collaboration by gaining access to the latest AI technologies and experiencing the benefits of cross-border innovation.

Students and young professionals are encouraged to participate in international cooperation in AI development to gain valuable experience and contribute to the future of technology. By engaging with peers from different countries, students can broaden their knowledge, develop new skills, and build a global network of collaborators. Young professionals can also benefit from international cooperation by advancing their careers, gaining exposure to diverse perspectives, and staying at the forefront of AI innovation.

Policymakers, economists, sociologists, parents, philosophers, ethicists, and the general public all have a role to play in fostering international cooperation in AI development. Policymakers can create frameworks and regulations that promote collaboration and ensure the responsible use of AI technology. Economists and sociologists can study the impact of international cooperation on AI development and its potential benefits for society. Parents can educate their children about the importance of global collaboration in technology. Philosophers and ethicists can explore the ethical implications of AI development in a global context. And the general public can support efforts to promote international cooperation in AI development for the betterment of society as a whole.

Harnessing the Potential of AI for Social Good

As we look towards the future of technology and artificial intelligence, it is important to consider how we can harness the potential of AI for social good. In today's world, AI has the power to transform industries, improve efficiency, and enhance our daily lives. But beyond simply making our lives easier, AI has the ability to address some of the most pressing social issues facing our world today.

One of the key ways in which AI can be used for social good is in the field of healthcare. By analyzing vast amounts of data, AI can help to identify patterns and trends in diseases, leading to earlier detection and more effective treatment options. AI can also be used to personalize healthcare, ensuring that each patient receives the individualized care they need. In this way, AI has the potential to revolutionize the healthcare industry and improve outcomes for patients around the world.

Another area where AI can have a significant impact is in education. By utilizing AI-powered tools, educators can provide personalized learning experiences for students, helping them to reach their full potential. AI can also help to identify struggling students early on, allowing for timely interventions and support. By harnessing the power of AI in education, we can ensure that all students have access to high-quality, individualized learning experiences.

In addition to healthcare and education. AI can also be used to address issues such as poverty, inequality, and climate change By analyzing data and identifying patterns AI can help policymakers and government officials make more informed decisions that benefit society as a whole. AI can also be used to optimize resource allocation, reduce waste and promote sustainability. By leveraging AI for social good we have the opportunity to create a more equitable and sustainable world for future generations.

As we move forward into the future of AI it is crucial that we consider how we can use this powerful technology for the betterment of society. By harnessing the potential of AI for social good we can address some of the most pressing challenges facing our world today From healthcare and education to poverty and climate change AI has the power to transform our world for the better It is up to all of us from software developers and policymakers to parents and philosophers. to work together to ensure that AI is used in a way that benefits all of humanity.

06

Chapter 6: Conclusion

Summary of Key Points

In this subchapter, we have summarized the key points discussed in "AI 2042: A Vision for Tomorrow's Technology" for our diverse audience. Whether you are a software developer, tech entrepreneur, gadget lover, student, policymaker, economist, parent, philosopher, or member of the general public, this summary will provide you with valuable insights into the future of artificial intelligence.

First and foremost, the book explores how AI technology has evolved beyond the realm of virtual assistants like Siri and self-driving cars. With advancements in machine learning, deep learning, and natural language processing, AI has the potential to revolutionize industries such as healthcare, finance, education, and transportation. The possibilities are endless, and it is crucial for stakeholders to stay informed and adapt to these changes.

One of the key takeaways from the book is the importance of ethical considerations in the development and deployment of AI technology. As AI becomes more integrated into our daily lives, it is essential to address issues such as bias, privacy, and accountability. Policymakers and government officials play a critical role in shaping regulations that protect the rights and well-being of individuals in the AI-driven world.

Furthermore, the book highlights the economic and societal implications of AI technology. From job automation and workforce displacement to the redistribution of wealth and power, AI has the potential to reshape the global economy and social structure. Economists and sociologists must anticipate these changes and propose solutions that ensure a fair and equitable future for all.

Lastly, the book emphasizes the importance of education and lifelong learning in the age of AI. Students and young professionals must acquire the necessary skills to thrive in a technology-driven world, while parents must prepare their children for a future where AI plays a central role. Philosophers and ethicists are also called upon to engage in discussions about the ethical implications of AI and guide societal values in the right direction. Overall, "AI 2042: A Vision for Tomorrow's Technology" provides a comprehensive look at the future of AI and encourages readers to think critically about the opportunities and challenges that lie ahead.

Looking Ahead to the Future of AI 2042

As we look ahead to the future of AI in 2042, it is clear that the possibilities are endless. From advancements in healthcare to improvements in transportation and communication, AI technology is set to revolutionize the way we live, work, and interact with the world around us. For software developers and programmers, this means new opportunities to create innovative solutions that can enhance our daily lives. Tech entrepreneurs will have the chance to capitalize on the growing demand for AI-driven products and services, while gadget lovers and early adopters can look forward to experiencing the latest in cutting-edge technology.

Students and young professionals entering the workforce in 2042 will find themselves in a world where AI plays an increasingly important role in nearly every industry. From finance to manufacturing, AI technology will have a profound impact on the way businesses operate and the skills required to succeed in the workforce. Policymakers and government officials will need to navigate the complex ethical and regulatory challenges that come with the widespread adoption of AI, ensuring that these technologies are used responsibly and in the best interest of society.

Economists and sociologists are already studying the potential economic and social implications of AI technology in 2042. From the impact on job markets to the distribution of wealth, AI has the power to reshape our society in ways we have yet to fully understand. Parents will need to prepare their children for a world where AI is an integral part of everyday life, teaching them the skills they need to thrive in a technology-driven society. Philosophers and ethicists will continue to grapple with the moral implications of AI, questioning the boundaries of machine intelligence and the implications for humanity.

For the general public, the future of AI in 2042 holds both promise and uncertainty. While AI has the potential to improve our lives in countless ways, it also raises important questions about privacy, security, and the nature of human intelligence. As we look ahead to the future of AI in 2042, it is crucial that we approach these technologies with a sense of curiosity and caution, ensuring that they are developed and deployed in a way that benefits us all. AI 2042 is not just about Siri and self driving cars - it is about shaping a future where AI technology enhances our lives in ways we never thought possible.

Call to Action for Stakeholders in the AI Ecosystem

In this subchapter, we issue a call to action for all stakeholders in the AI ecosystem to come together and shape the future of technology for the betterment of society. As software developers and programmers, you have the power to create innovative AI solutions that can revolutionize the way we live and work. Your expertise and creativity are crucial in advancing AI technology beyond simple virtual assistants like Siri and self driving cars.

Tech entrepreneurs and gadget lovers, you have the vision and resources to bring these AI innovations to market and drive adoption among consumers. By investing in AI research and development, you can help accelerate the pace of technological progress and unlock new opportunities for growth and prosperity.

Students and young professionals, now is the time to immerse yourselves in the world of AI and gain the skills and knowledge needed to thrive in this rapidly evolving field. By pursuing education and training in AI, you can position yourselves for success and make a meaningful impact on the future of technology.

Policymakers and government officials, your decisions and regulations will play a critical role in shaping the ethical and societal implications of AI technology. It is imperative that you work collaboratively with industry stakeholders to establish guidelines and frameworks that promote responsible AI development and deployment.

Economists, sociologists, parents, philosophers, ethicists, and the general public, your perspectives and input are invaluable in ensuring that AI technology serves the greater good and upholds ethical standards. By engaging in discussions and debates about the implications of AI, you can help shape a future where technology enhances our lives while respecting our values and principles. Together, we can harness the power of AI to create a brighter and more inclusive tomorrow for all.

A.I. 2042: Beyond Self-Driving Cars - The Shocking Future You Don't Know (But Should!)

Forget Self-Driving Cars, What's Next for AI? **AI 2042** takes you beyond the headlines and explores the cutting edge of AI research. We're not just talking song suggestions and self-driving cars anymore! **This book is for you if:** * **You're fascinated by technology**:

Delve into the race for Artificial General Intelligence (AGI) - a machine that could surpass human intelligence! * **You're curious about the future**: Explore how AI could revolutionize space exploration, unlock groundbreaking scientific discoveries, and even colonize other planets! * **You're concerned about the impact**:

We tackle the complex issue of automation and the future of work. But don't worry, we also explore how AI can create new job opportunities. **But AI isn't all sunshine and rainbows.** This book also examines the ethical dilemmas of superintelligence and explores how we can ensure AI benefits humanity. *

*Whether you're an AI enthusiast, a concerned citizen, or simply curious about the future, AI 2042 equips you with the knowledge to navigate this exciting and complex world.**

Ready to unlock the potential of AI? **Click "Buy Now" and start your AI adventure today!**

www.ingramcontent.com/pod-product-compliance
Lightning Source LLC
LaVergne TN
LVHW051751050326
832903LV00029B/2851